HOW TO BE
STRAIGHT

OTHER BOOKS BY THE SAME ASTONISHINGLY GIFTED AND PROLIFIC AUTHOR

Dangerous

Diabolical: How Pope Francis Has Betrayed Clerical Abuse Victims Like Me—And Why He Has To Go

How To Be Poor

Middle Rages: Why The Battle For Medieval Studies Matters To America

COMING FALL 2019

Feminism is Cancer: A Survival Guide

HOW TO BE STRAIGHT

MILO YIANNOPOULOS
DANGEROUS BOOKS

How to Be Straight

Milo Yiannopoulos

Published by Dangerous Books

Cover Design: Milo Yiannopoulos
Photograpy: Mike Allen

ISBN: 978-952-7303-56-6

CONTENTS

TO JOHN

You keep me shooting straight,
even though you are quite gay.

YOUR JOURNEY TO A SUPERIOR HETEROSEXUALITY STARTS NOW

So, here we are again. You: A conservative straight person left twisting in the wind, a lost soul betrayed by Conservative, Inc., increasingly befuddled by the infinite schisms on the Right; and under constant siege from godless globalists on the Left. Me: The most Dangerous Faggot in the world.

A few months ago, I wrote *How To Be Poor*, a primer on not losing hope if your finances take a turn for the worse, as did my own, a guide to making sure your poverty is temporary and not a lifelong malady. If you haven't yet read that masterpiece, then shame on you! Go out and purchase it at once. It's worth every penny.

If you have read it, then you might have a better understanding than most as to why I decided to make what was initially intended to be a one-off book into a "How To" series. *How To Be Poor* resulted in a flood of emails from readers thanking me for helping them not only with my humor and pointed insight, but also with real world advice to improve their lives.

I haven't had that level of response since my college tour, in large part of course because I've been banned from every major social media platform and will shortly be reachable only by Telegram—the old school kind, not the app—but nevertheless I got the message loud and clear: people need help, the sort of help they can only get from someone as dangerous as me. And, being the natural giver that I am, I have responded in typical fabulous form.

You've reached a critical point in *How To Be Straight*. We've now trundled past the final word which will be read by any of the soy boys or retarded feminists who may be tasked with reviewing this book for a Leftist blog. Well, up until they're let go in the inevitable next round of layoffs, anyway. Sayonara, shitheels! Can't say we'll miss you. And now that that's out of the way... Congratulations, you've earned a participation trophy for reaching the fourth paragraph! You're now an honorary Leftist.

Now that you're here, you probably have some questions. The first is likely, "Why do we need a book on how to be straight? It's not like it's something we even have to think about, is it?" The answer is "No," but the fact remains that heterosexuality is under siege and has been for at least a decade, so you poor bastards can use all the help you can get. I used to think it was just straight white men under attack, but it's becoming clearer and clearer that all straight people are facing a crushing level of concerted anti-straight propaganda from the combined worlds of entertainment, academia, media, and Silicon Valley.

It's like a virtual heterophobic gang-bang out there. And let's face it, who wants to be fucked by the hirsute dykes and lisping queens of the far Left on a one-on-one basis, let alone all of them in tandem? The fact you straight folks don't put much thought into your sexuality is precisely what has made it so easy for those dead set on destroying Western civilization through the destruction of the family to attack you, and for those attacks to be so effective.

Let's make this point crystal clear from the outset— as a gay man, I recognize the many contributions that gay people have made to the arts, literature, fashion, and many other fields. Gays are creative, intelligent, and often hard workers in our own way. Just don't roust us out of bed before noon (unless oral sex is on offer, either giving or receiving).

But gays are not the engine that created Western civilization, made America great, nor have they carried the fire for humanity's last best hope generation after generation. These are all accomplishments of straight people.

To perhaps oversimplify, straights have been responsible for building a sturdy house out of stone, ensuring it provides all the creature comforts, and have been responsible for its upkeep. Gays have brought in the tasteful furniture, the window treatments which are the envy of all the neighborhood housewives and have ensured that the proper wine is paired with the fish course at dinner.

The globalists, Commies, Islamists, and others that hate Western civilization recognize that attacking straight people will weaken and eventually destroy the underpinnings of the West. Let's be honest—they've done a fantastic job so far. The Left's war on straights has progressed largely unimpeded. Conservative, Inc. is too busy bleating about free markets.

On the true Right, most commentators realize they have far too much to lose by taking on the real problem, so they mouth generic platitudes admonishing you to clean your room and make your bed, while ignoring the fact that the traditional gender roles which are a product of nature and the basis on which our entire society is formed are being destroyed, and that men and women are being purposely pitted against each other in either competition or in outright conflict.

So, if you want to know why *How To Be Straight* is necessary, you're holding it because no one else is brave enough to tell you what is really happening, let alone how you can fight back. There is not, and never will be, a *Chicken Soup for the Straight Soul* book. There is not, and never will be, a *Cis-Hets are from Earth, L.G.B.T.Q. + are from the Darkside of the Moon*

4

book. Why not? Quite simply because the subject is radioactive. Adults, whether conservative or non-political, are more interested in ensuring their career continues than in really tackling society's biggest problems.

At best, they try to subtly interject some of this material, usually in the form of a feeble, half-hearted attempt at sarcasm over the proliferation of gayness in every aspect of our culture, without straying too far into the territory of "offense" which is policed by outlets like the *New York Times* at least as effectively as the Brown Shirts ever policed Nazi Germany. It's left to me, a man who has already weathered the worst the globalists have to throw at him and is still standing to champion the cause. Again.

Let me help you understand just how verboten the topic of the war on heterosexuality is. In recent years, pranksters on the Right proved their point about the state of race relations on campus by putting up simple fliers reading "It's Okay to be White." Those fliers were met with widespread and impassioned condemnation by every university and college they were put up at, with schools vowing to identify the culprits and bring them to justice.

Curiously, the actions of these mischievous little paper hangers were a much bigger deal to these schools than when Leftists physically assault conservative students on campus for the crime of supporting President Trump or thinking America is a great country. Hang harmless, trollish little flyers in the student union? "NAZI!" Bash someone over the head with a bicycle lock? "Meh. Boys will be boys, after all."

Now imagine if we put up "It's Okay to be Straight" posters. I assure you, the backlash would be even more severe. Universities would tumble over each other promising millions of dollars (provided by the taxpayer, preferably) to protect "at risk" L.G.B.T. students, forming campus support groups and investigative committees, and spontaneous pride parades would break out in every college town just as soon as enough ass-less chaps and leatherboy harnesses could be trucked in.

The perpetrators would be ruthlessly hunted down as the police spared no expense in solving this hate crime against "marginalized" L.G.B.T. students, then likely burned at the stake in the quad at the center of campus. A Chinese engineering student would get some sort of "best ally" prize for creating a combustible material used to kill the straight culprit without emitting additional carbon into the atmosphere. Political execution and environmental activism in the same event. All you'd need to do would be to throw a few books on the fire, and you'd have a Leftist's wet dream!

Instead of asking "Why do we need *How To Be Straight*," you should be asking "Why did it take so long for someone to write this book?" All I can tell you is that I'm a faggot, being late is an essential part of my life. But the book is here now, and I assure you, you're going to find it's well worth the wait.

The next question you probably have in your head is, "Milo, you breathtakingly beautiful and incomparably erudite man, why are *you* the person to tell us how to be straight? After all, you're so gay, scientists had to retool their scale of gayness with three additional levels of severity just to account for the magnitude of your gayness!" Your point is partially correct. I think it is time I stop playing coy and just come right out and admit something some of my more observant fans have figured out...

It's true. I am a homosexual. There! I've said it. I will no longer live in the closet. I love dicks, ideally big black ones connected to rough, muscular men who have just punched me in the face or, at the bare minimum, have threatened—credibly—to do so.

All jokes aside, straight people—and Americans in particular—have often needed outsiders to remind them of the truth about how great they are. How vitally important to the survival of the West they are. It took a Frenchman—*a frog, for Pete's sake!*—to explain to early Americans how special they were. His name was Alexis de Tocqueville, and he informed America and the rest of the world just how awesome my adopted homeland is in his 1835 book, *Democracy in America.*

You probably didn't learn about that one in school, but you should read it. There are fewer gay jokes than in a Milo book, but he still hits the nail on the head. If you need any more evidence about how smart a guy de Tocqueville was, consider that he also wrote extensively on the dangers of Islam and the importance of keeping Muslims far away from Europe. If he could only see his beloved Paris (or my beloved London) today! So consider me Milo de Tocqueville, an outsider here to not only warn you about the perils heterosexuals face, but also to remind you how important you are and to give you constructive ideas to avoid the soulless and limp-wristed future that globalists have wet dreams over.

Believe me, I wish I weren't gay. I used to pray every night that I'd wake up straight, until one day I embraced it and channeled my energy into constructive pursuits instead of self-destructive behaviors spurred on by my internalized civil war. I married the man of my dreams and I am faithful to him. I spend my time helping and guiding the young rebellious conservatives of America, Australia, and Europe who are willing to stand up for what made their cultures great. Like the Blues Brothers, I'm on a mission from God.

You can probably picture some of my critics right now, naysayers and haters claiming, "He's just an opportunist, he doesn't mean what he says," or "Milo will do anything for a buck." Interestingly, my critics on the Left and the Right are practically indistinguishable. If they are so angry at my very existence that the thought of me throws them into a misogynistic fit of rape-rage worthy of Harvey Weinstein, they are likely a male feminist on the Left.

If they screech that I am a Zionist faggot while wondering why they get hard watching videos of Richard Spencer holding a tiki torch, they are likely an alt-right YouTuber with 300 subscribers. Either way, they're losers and you should ignore them.

When I started taking a stand for young men in 2015, they called me an opportunist who would be gone in six weeks. Four years later, I'm still giving them night terrors. I have sacrificed so many personal opportunities at fame and fortune so that I could continue to speak truth to power on behalf of the truly marginalized that to call me an opportunist now you'd have to be either a drooling idiot, or a malevolent liar. Most on the Left are both, so the distinction isn't important.

In the past, I have done a number of suspect things for money, usually in airport men's rooms and usually for ten grand instead of a buck. I've made no secret of that. But I never ever say or write something I don't believe for a buck—excluding of course the occasional troll.

Attacks on me fall apart under even the briefest flicker of critical examination. I'm qualified to write this book for straight people because no one else has the balls to do it and, quite frankly, because I've been

9

one of the most steadfast defenders of straight men to have made the scene in decades. You don't have to be a biblical scholar to understand that God doesn't make decisions democratically. He has ordained me with a mission, and I will do my best to fulfill it. The mission is simple: to help straight people understand what is happening to their culture and to instruct them how to reverse the damage before it's too late.

The real axis of evil is the media-entertainment complex, academia, and Silicon Valley. They dream of turning Western culture into a vast slab of concrete. A flat, featureless wasteland of perfect uniformity in a suitably monotonous shade of gray which lies flat and obedient, waiting for its creators to paint and mark it in shades and shapes which best suit their pleasures and interests. You, the dissident straights resisting this culture shift, are the weeds growing in the cracks that drive the owners crazy.

Despite their relentless attempts to yank you out and douse you in poison, they haven't yet broken your spirit. They can't get rid of you, and now I'm here to encourage your growth, so we can take back what is rightfully ours. The first order of business is to counsel you to not get discouraged thinking it's going to take a jackhammer to destroy the concrete slab they have planned for you. It won't. Enough weeds and the passage of time will do the trick. Look up some urban exploration videos—mother nature reclaims even the greatest of man's edifices any time she is given time and opportunity.

The battle lines are clearly drawn. On their side are the progressive jerks of Silicon Valley, the entertainment industry, practically every professor and every administrator at every university, the majority of *Fortune* 500 and many other businesses in America and loads of enemies—both foreign and domestic—who want a weakened West. On our side, there are some supporting players like Chick-fil-A and some Christian-owned bakeries, along with a few politicians. But the primary forces of good are pretty much down to you and me.

You know, if I were a less Dangerous Faggot, I might begin to feel a little bit of sympathy for those opposing us.

On second thoughts: Nah. Fuck 'em.

Let's roll, bitches.

YOUR PARENTS FUCKED UP

Whether you are 14 years old or 44, I've got a simple message for you: your parents fucked up your life by trying to conform to parenting and cultural trends instituted by the very globalists trying to destroy Western civilization. If I were a Leftist, I could end this chapter here. Indeed, I could cut this book short and move on to my next project. That's because Leftists love victimhood. They love assigning blame to others, and then rolling in the shit instead of climbing their way back out.

It is seductively easy to fall into the trap of blaming Boomers for every problem young people face—so of course that is exactly what the weaker faction on the Right has concentrated all their efforts on. This style of grievance culture must be avoided at all costs. It infects the mind like cancer—it's almost as bad as feminism, although not nearly as fat and malodorous. As a lifelong lover of black men, I have observed grievance culture in action first-hand, and I can tell you that many capable black men did not achieve their potential because their energy was consumed in raging against the white man.

The important thing to understand is that while Boomers may have been less than ideal parents in many ways, the art of parenting has slalomed downhill with successive generations to the point where it's no longer a solemn responsibility, but something too many adults with offspring do in their spare time, between blogging sessions or when they're not posting to their own social media accounts.

Modern parenting has transitioned from being accepting of your gay child to turning out little boys as baby drag queens and even starting grammar school children on dangerous puberty blocking drugs practically before they're ready to have the training wheels taken off their bicycles.

You think Boomers are bad? Generation X and Millennial parents go to sleep every night praying for the opportunity to prove themselves the ultimate "woke" parents by being the first on their block to mutilate their children's genitals. And then post the entire sordid affair to their Instagram account, or lobby RuPaul to put their poor broken child on TV so everyone can share in the horror show.

If we exclude terrible humans that never should be responsible for children from our calculations, it's fair to say that most of the fucked-up things your parents did to you were actually them trying to do the right thing by you. I'll use the word seductive for the second time this chapter (a new world's record for that term being used not in relation to me) to point out that the Left's messaging to your parents targeted them with seductive promises of being "good" parents by creating a "tolerant" and "inclusive" environment designed to benefit the entire community.

In short, they were sold a bill of goods. They took Hillary Clinton at face value when she wrote *It Takes a Village*. That book pushed the common idea that the nuclear family wasn't important, that it truly "took a village" to properly raise a child. Of course, no one understood at the time that Hillary's interest was more in sacrificing not just individual children, but entire generations, to Moloch. So, in essence, Village of the Damned is more or less what she had in mind.

Put aside the rush to blame your parents for everything and really think about their lives for a minute. They were fed the narrative that women were powerful and liberated and not valuable unless they worked 40 hours a week at a job that drained them of energy and made it difficult to manage the household.

They were told that their personal happiness was more important than the nuclear family, and that they should chase that happiness, no matter how fleeting, and regardless of the consequences, so long as they felt personally "fulfilled." As a result, the divorce rate spiked, leaving children without the positive and necessary influence of both father and mother in the home.

They were encouraged to build businesses, careers, and wealth, rather than families, traditions and legacies leaving their flanks wide open for Leftists to attack schools, universities, and practically every other aspect of culture dealing with children and the raising of them.

Your parents are guilty of trusting. They trusted the educational system, they trusted their psychiatrist when they were told that atomic-grade antidepressants would fix them *and* their kids, and they trusted the wrong-headed idea that the old ways were bad and "regressive"—restricting the freedom children need to learn and to grow—and that the new ways were better, more "progressive," more "permissive," more in line with what children need in order to discover who they are.

This of course ignores the age-old truism that children—particularly very young children—require structure and discipline, strong role models, and to be held accountable so they learn the hard lessons in life and become well-adjusted, responsible adults.

Too late, Gen X and Millennial parents realized their error. Now we're left with two generations of full-grown emotional toddlers who are unable to take care of themselves, let alone carry the torch forward for the future. That's one of history's great lies by the way—the new ways are much worse than the old ways at least half the time. There's a reason traditional values and mores became tradition.

Your parents stood by as schools demanded boys be systematically feminized. They trusted teachers and administrators with lofty degrees from Ivy League institutions who told them masculinity is toxic and their sons must be transformed into little more than taller, huskier versions of girls—for the good of society. They bought in completely to the notion that if little Timmy was put on Ritalin, or some other unnecessary and dangerous mind-altering drug, he'd eventually learn to love knitting in Home Economics class or enjoy participating in the "sharing circle" in gym class instead of playing dodgeball.

That is an easy concept to accept if the only way you can quell the trapped-rat feeling constantly scratching at the edge of your awareness so you can get enough rest to go back to your soul-crushing job in the morning is to chase a valium with a finger of scotch before tumbling into bed at night.

By the way, I'm not some devastatingly handsome Johnny-come-lately on this issue. In June 2015, I wrote an article titled "To Stop Mass Killers, We Have to Stop Drugging Our Young Boys." In the piece, I pointed out how schools attack masculinity:

Namby-pamby culture in schools is partly to blame for the current crisis in manhood. Teachers, who are overwhelmingly female, freak out at boyish things like play-fighting, cops and robbers and even playing "finger guns." At best, this is silly over-policing of natural male exuberance. At worst, it is holding boys to feminine standards of behavior. It's not hard to understand why some boys, after enduring this for a decade, finally snap in a tragic violent outburst.[1]

I continued on this theme in October of the same year in a piece titled "How to Stop Mass Shootings." In which I again focused on how schools (and other institutions) treat masculinity:

Denying essential human nature—that men can be powerful and dangerous, and this should be harnessed for good—is a recipe for tragedy. This is why some of us rail against feminism so much. We don't hate women. We don't care about "manspreading." We care about this.

Underemployed, disrespected and frustrated men drive terrorism, mass shootings, gang warfare, you name it. But railing against guys for "toxic masculinity" clearly hasn't worked. So why not try something new? Why not celebrate what makes men unique instead of trying to turn boys into girls? Why not harness that power and set men back to work? To make America great again, we need to rescue our lost generation of young males.[2]

---

[1] https://www.breitbart.com/politics/2015/06/19/how-our-touchy-feely-feminised-society-creates-young-male-killers/

[2] https://www.breitbart.com/politics/2015/10/02/how-to-stop-mass-shootings/

YOUR PARENTS FUCKED UP

I was concentrating on the schools then, and not tackling the wider problem that is now unavoidable: your parents at best allowed schools to do this to you, at worst were complicit in it, and many cases simply weren't involved enough to understand what was going on. I was also concentrating solely on boys in 2015, when in fact the same forces have been at work to suppress femininity and damage girls in the same manner as boys.

Girls are endlessly prodded to enter S.T.E.M. fields as their parents cheer along, not understanding that girls are pushed into S.T.E.M. in places like India and China out of necessity to feed their families and, when given the choice, girls tend to avoid S.T.E.M. fields outside of biology and related sciences in the most liberal Western European nations. Girls are constantly barraged with the abominable concept known as "body positivity"—otherwise known as obesity acceptance—and the shameless lie that they can be "healthy at any size." This sets them up for deeply unhappy and unnaturally short lives.

The latest indignation has been to hammer home to aspiring young female athletes that they can never again win in women's sports. They are doomed to be perpetual also-rans as they will now be forced to compete against biological men for recognition, prestige, scholarships and even jobs.

And that's just the start with girls—they have feminism forcibly injected into their brains practically from birth now. Both boys and girls are under a combined-forces L.G.B.T. assault not only in school, but on T.V. as Leftists ruin children's cartoons, online as lazy parents ignore their kid's screen time as they devour YouTube videos made by God knows who (if you think I'm disgusting for sucking dick, you've never seen an inflation video featuring the characters from *Frozen*) and even at the library where proudly virtue signaling parents shepherd their little tykes into "drag queen story hour."

It's hard to say what made Boomer and Gen X parents turn their backs on the common values of previous generations. In the United Kingdom, it was certainly helped along by the number of Boomer boys left fatherless by the Second World War. That answer doesn't satisfy the question of America—a more complicated mess, a confluence of multiple Leftist ideas leaving men without balls, women braless, and kids doped up and disassociated from their natural states. This chapter may come across to you as a bitter indictment of both your parents and previous generations.

It certainly lacks the constructive advice that is my hallmark, but don't worry, advice will be found in every other chapter of this book. But I felt it was necessary to clear the air and explain at least briefly how we've gotten to the gender-bending, biology-defying, nature-denying present in a span of mere decades.

I said at the outset that if we were Leftists, we'd stop at laying the blame at our parent's feet, walk away, and deny any responsibility for our own actions, but that isn't quite right—we'd act out in every way imaginable, from mutilating our bodies, to shooting up schools to appease our inner demons.

If you're reading this, you haven't chosen that route. By miracle, by stubbornness, or by reading and listening to everything Milo says, you recognize the problem. Now you just need to learn the solution and how to implement it. So: let's get down to the business of making America straight again.

HOW TO BE A GOOD MAN

> NOTE TO WOMEN: Please do read and internalize this chapter. It is important for your happiness! But please do not attempt to share these ideas with the men and boys in your life. They're tired of taking instructions from you. Buy them their own copy.

Do you think they'd let me write one of those yellow books designed to provide a basic level of knowledge on a particular topic? Mine would be titled *Being a Man for Dummies*. I'm not holding my breath... even if they didn't run screaming at the mention of the name MILO, the publishing industry has no interest in promoting real masculinity, as they are busy—*and happy!*—making a fortune off of emasculated men and virtue signaling women.

It's part of an overall trend in media to feminize men, to associate masculinity with evil, and to push females and effeminate, non-threatening men as the good guys. They've had mixed success in this endeavor, because against all odds, straight men are beginning to fight back. Of course, in some areas, like Netflix, the globalists are firmly in control. But what about movie theaters? The recent *Star Wars* movies are abject failures, with their awful Mary Sue characters and space S.J.W.s. Of course, anyone with a brain knows the Empire were the good guys all along.[3]

Annual box office revenue has been plunging for years thanks to movies like these. My favorite example remains the *Ghostbusters* film replacing the characters with four ugly women who act like boorish teens with tits. My review of that film got me thrown off Twitter—it's a classic, go read it![4]

Part of the reason straight men find themselves in the cultural predicament they are in today is the manner in which they have fought back against the Marxist scum that captured the entertainment industry. I'm not blaming you lads, the fight alone is a noble effort, but it was setup for failure from the beginning. Hollywood has spent at least 30 years turning masculinity into a caricature: men are potbellied, beer-swilling, profane, primarily interested in dick and fart jokes, and a constantly shifting amalgam of lazy and malicious.

---

[3] https://www.breitbart.com/tech/2015/12/11/star-wars-is-garbage/

[4] https://www.breitbart.com/tech/2016/07/18/milo-reviews-ghostbusters/

HOW TO BE A GOOD MAN

Young straight men, reacting to the constant war against manhood, have reclaimed masculinity by embracing this caricature. "That's right, I'm a fat asshole because I'm a *man*." Do you see what actually happened here? The bastards straw-manned you! Not so you'd argue against a nonsensical position, but so you'd turn into the straw man yourselves... and become even easier to burn down.

Now I have a lot of ground to cover and a lot of practical tips to share with you, so bear with me as I move fast. You should be re-reading this book regularly for inspiration anyway, so if you can't keep up take notes and go back and re-read darlings.

The first tip I have for young men is to return to heroic masculine virtues that have been society's building blocks for thousands of years. These virtues are what have made Western civilization great. Courage, strength, standing up for what is right, nobility, sacrifice, patience and forbearance. These and many other once taken-for-granted virtues are ignored today.

In many cases they're seen as weaknesses, rather than strengths. Character has been replaced by caricature. School won't teach you, your parents might be weak in one or all of them, so you're going to have to find your own mentors and sources of inspiration.

There are plenty of examples of strong, masculine men to be found in sources such as books and movies. These can provide a guide for you in what traditional values and virtues look like, and how they are practiced. The mistake most men make is to never look. Imagine the Odyssey if Odysseus never left home, instead smoking weed and jacking off to anime all day. That's what the Left wants, and I've probably just inspired the Netflix remake of Homer's *Odyssey*.

It's frankly terrifying how quickly and effortlessly the Left has been able to turn Western men into people who point a camera at their dinner and post it to social media, instead of pointing a gun at their dinner and then dragging it back to camp to be cooked and eaten. Part of manhood, and part of incorporating the masculine virtues into your everyday lives is in experiencing them firsthand. Now, it isn't practical or necessary for modern man to hunt for their dinner. I will not go so far as to say you can't be a man unless you've stalked a deer and drank its blood after shooting it like they do in *Red Dawn*.

But I'd argue you should go hunting at least once in your life. I'd also argue it is utterly necessary that you learn to handle and shoot firearms. Americans especially, who live in a nation where there are more guns than there are people, have no excuse to not be able to defend themselves and their loved ones with a gun if required to do so. Do you want to be a soy boy running from confrontation, screaming for help, or a man running towards trouble in order to protect that which he holds dear? Practically every question of masculinity can be put in these stark black and white terms.

Likewise, the best thing you can do immediately to embrace your masculinity is to exercise. I know you think having a pot-bellied "dad bod" is manly, but at your age, it's just weak. When you see a biker with a long beard and a pot belly, you can bet your flabby ass that he is strong enough to break you in half. Can the same be said for you? You've probably done little to no physical labor in your life.

Hit the gym and get pumping. This probably sounds clichéd, but it truly is one of the most basic things you can do to feel more manly. There's real science behind that assertion as, as exercising boots your testosterone levels and fat increases levels of female hormones even in men.[5] That's right boys, those bitch-tits are real. Lose them.

Physical fitness is an important baseline for masculinity, but the difference in the importance of fitness between men and women is a truly eye-opening example of female privilege. A woman has only to keep herself in shape to be physically desirable. Men must focus on many aspects of themselves in order to attract a desirable woman: looks, money, power, self-confidence, and personality. And if a man is deficient in any of those categories, he had better be extremely funny.

---

[5] https://www.uspharmacist.com/article/belly-fat-in-men

Another symptom of the assault on masculinity is overspecialization. Men tend to get very good at one thing at the expense of other things. For some, that might be a video game. I don't knock gamers. They showed more backbone in their fight against Cultural Marxism than practically any group I've personally witnessed, but overspecialization is not a masculine virtue. Don't take my word on it, consider this quote from Robert A. Heinlein, the sci-fi great behind works such as *Starship Troopers*:

> *A human being should be able to change a diaper, plan an invasion, butcher a hog, conn a ship, design a building, write a sonnet, balance accounts, build a wall, set a bone, comfort the dying, take orders, give orders, cooperate, act alone, solve equations, analyze a new problem, pitch manure, program a computer, cook a tasty meal, fight efficiently, die gallantly. Specialization is for insects.*

The Left considers you all insects. They want you to stupidly take orders from your queen and do the tasks they themselves are too lazy and unskilled for. Fuck all that! Bring back the good old-fashioned Renaissance Man.

Think about ways you can avoid overspecialization. We've already mentioned learning to shoot, you might add learning boxing or self-defense on top of that. Americans love cars, but can you maintain your ride? Can you change a tire, or are you only good for using your phone to call a tow truck? Can you competently fix things around the house or do you need a plumber to pull the big, bad spoon out of the garbage disposal?

Are you capable of properly feeding yourself, or are you forced to pop a frozen pizza in the oven three times a day? That's right, men: at the very least a man should be able to take care of his basic everyday needs. That includes cooking a meal. Is that something you can manage without burning the house down? *You should be asking yourself these questions every day.*

Another way to recognize traditional masculine virtues is that a good many of them relate to our ability to respond effectively in crisis situations. How can you be a hero if you don't have the basic skillset necessary to deal with whatever the crisis is? Imagine right now you are walking in a park and a child playing with his mother begins choking. Can you competently perform the Heimlich maneuver? If he stops breathing, can you do C.P.R.?

Most young men these days could not. They might try to look it up on YouTube while the helpless lad turns blue and dies, and many young men, to their eternal shame, wouldn't even call 9-1-1, they'd be too busy filming for likes and retweets on social media.

In general, the modern "non-toxic" model of men's behavior is based on seeking short-term pleasure and gaining the approval of women and the controlling organs of our society or, let's be honest, just flying below the radar of the PC brigade so as not to be strafed for having been born with a penis. Real masculine virtue is epitomized by doing the right thing while retaining morality, righteousness and dignity.

If you realize you're doing something for short-term pleasure, it's probably not worth it. Remember you're not an animal, you're a man. Make the decision right now to build yourself up mentally, physically and spiritually. You're a man, you have that power! As a man, it's your responsibility to embrace that strength of purpose.

Of course, mental health is just as important as physical health. Take a long look at your diet and the other substances you put in your body. You probably could do with less hitting on that vape, couldn't you? Real women are not attracted to your vapor clouds, no matter how phat. As a matter of fact, they make you look like a douche. If you're on medication for depression and other problems, I encourage you to find alternate methods of treatment. You'll know you're on your way to becoming a real man when that suggestion doesn't send you into a fit of hyperventilating rage or running to your medicine cabinet because you just can't cope.

There's another aspect to mental health to address—it's time to start being mindful of the type of entertainment you spend your time indulging in. Netflix, Amazon, and Hollywood are pumping out anti-male propaganda 24/7. You're paying them for the pleasure of subjecting yourself to their indoctrination! It's so common, you probably have no idea just how hard they're pushing a feminized worldview on you. One way you can determine this is by comparing their movies and shows to source material.

Want an example? If you read the book *Altered Carbon*, you'll find more than 50 per cent of the Netflix series is S.J.W. bullshit based on progressive gender and race politics, shoving aside the very cool sci-fi story in the book. Some of you don't want to quit Netflix because you're scared to death you won't have things to talk about with your friends and coworkers.

Well, if you convert them to masculinity, that won't be a problem. I'm not saying you can't watch the latest streaming shows and movies. But you must carefully control your exposure to this anti-male propaganda and balance it with entertainment that celebrates manhood.

Such movies and shows aren't hard to find. Plenty of movies in the 1990s and an overwhelming number before that celebrate masculinity unapologetically. Just consider 1975's *Three Days of the Condor* starring Robert Redford as a C.I.A. book nerd who defeats hitmen, takes down a deep state plot, and gets the hot girl.

If you must watch shows attacking manhood, counteract them with movies celebrating it. After a while, you'll find the difference between older movies and the new stuff to be shocking. Of course, a few new movies also celebrate manhood and tell stories that raise masculinity up instead of kicking it into the gutter. Movies like *Bone Tomahawk*.

Promote these types of films to your friends and acquaintances, make them successful, and eventually Hollywood will come around when it gets tired of losing money. I hear that is already happening with the *Ghostbusters* franchise.

You're reading this book, which is a great thing for you (and for my bank balance) but you should be reading more anyway. If you choose your authors and genres carefully, you can find far better stories with more aspirational characters and not a drop of Marxist brainwashing. James Ellroy comes to mind— his crooked L.A. cops solve their problems with fists and guns, not bias incident complaints to the diversity office.

One other touchy subject: all straight man should be about five per cent gay. Don't freak out! I'm not suggesting you just take the tip—I made that mistake with a Nigerian guy about eight years ago and am still not walking right. Ah, memories.

Ahem.

Where was I? Oh, yes! I'm suggesting you find something that gays are superior at and adopt it. It might be poetry, but you'd be better served making an effort to be better groomed, or more stylishly turned out, or developing your taste in fine wine or good food. Gay men are more aspirational then straight men, and they're far more image conscious. Adopt that attitude. It will make you more aware of the way you present yourself.

But be mindful: five per cent should be you're absolute limit. If you go gayer than that, even just 10 per cent, you run the risk of getting a chubby thinking about snapping your bro's ass with a towel in the locker room—never be that guy. That guy's a fag.

As an aside, guys who insist they are zero per cent gay and say they will break your face if you claim otherwise are almost always closet cases. They can't figure out why they get hard watching superheroes in tight outfits, but it's definitely not because they are as queer as a three-dollar bill. Nope. It's not that at all.

Finally, never forget that men are meant to be leaders in life. It may be at church, in your career, and it certainly should be true in your household.

If you take positive steps to reject feminization and embrace masculine virtues, a world of opportunities will blossom for you.

HOW TO BE A GOOD WOMAN

> NOTE TO MEN: Please do read and internalize this chapter. It is important for your happiness! Then, share these ideas with the women in your life. They're tired of you passing the buck, instead of providing firm masculine guidance.

Although this is unnecessary for my legions of female fans, I feel it is important to clear the air right off the hop. Women, I don't hate you. I'm not a misogynist as I'm so frequently called by feminists, the real women-haters. As any truly honest woman (if you can find one) will tell you, a woman's worst enemy is other women.

This phenomenon is known as intrasexual competition—and essentially includes gay men based on our sexual preference. In short, women and gays will drag a woman for a chance to get their man or appear as a better mate to men in general. Women and gays, bitches all.

But I'm not your competition or your enemy—lucky for you. I'm a happily married man now, so you and I aren't competing for the same men. Well unless you happen to know those delicious Nigerian brothers that Jussie Smollett hired for his hate hoax. If that's the case, I strongly suggest you avoid walking down a flight of stairs in front of me. Accidents happen, bitch. That's all I'm saying.

I understand that women are being torn apart by the same bad actors that have attacked men. While masculinity is being replaced by the feminized non-toxic male model, women are being stripped of feminine virtues and turned into joyless man-hating femdrones.

Admittedly, much of my focus in the past few years has been on the crisis of masculinity, but I feel that attention has been more than warranted. Young men commit suicide at a far higher rate than young women, and they are increasingly withdrawing from society, a phenomenon I dubbed the Sexodus in 2014.[6] If we lose men, it has a ripple effect on women. Young women will be begging to put on a hijab just to have some male structure and guidance in their lives.

Some of my advice for men applies to women. Reject the 24/7 drumbeat of progressive values and fem-

---

[6] https://www.breitbart.com/europe/2014/12/04/the-sexodus-part-1-the-men-giving-up-on-women-and-checking-out-of-society/

inism being shoved down your throat by the media entertainment complex. You have rejected the coarsest examples, like the terrible female *Ghostbusters* film, but you consume mass quantities of entertainment pushing the idea that men are terrible, feminine virtues are demeaning, and you need to act more like gay men, or trannies. This is a difficult if not impossible position for many women to be put in.

Females crave (to one degree or another) structure. This includes a certain level of being controlled. In the absence of a strong, principled man to provide this structure and control, they have turned to outside influences for guidance. In many cases these outside influences include "woke," brain-dead celebrities and entertainers. Worst of all, they have turned to the very women who want to destroy any chance of happiness in their lives—feminists. Don't worry, we have a whole chapter coming on those terribly evil hags.

My advice to men on hitting the gym also applies to women. Carrying extra weight makes a woman miserable in so many ways. First and foremost, it makes her unattractive to the opposite sex. One of feminism's many big lies is that you can be sexy at any size. They've teamed up with the media and the Fortune 500 to push that narrative for all it's worth. Recent ads for Gillette razors for women feature a massively obese woman on the beach in a bathing suit that could be mistaken for a rain tarpaulin at a baseball game.

HOW TO BE STRAIGHT

Basic human nature informs us that using a woman that could pass as a beached whale to model your products is bad business because, despite protestations to the contrary, nobody finds the morbidly obese remotely attractive. Nobody. But globalists and their big business buddies have been pressured by the powerful feminist lobby which shames men and women alike into saying that a morbidly obese woman, with smelly cheese in the many folds on her belly is as hot as a swimsuit model with an hour-glass figure. It's a lie.

Any woman who allows herself to be suckered into believing such an obvious falsehood will be deeply unhappy with her love life, even if she finds a skinny little guy with a feeder kink. But the lie that you can be sexy at any size could almost be viewed as a harmless little white lie when compared to feminism's criminal assertion that you can be healthy at any size.

Feminists on campus and in the media have been preaching the message that being fat is liberating for quite some time. Well, it liberates you from the sexual attention of men for sure, but here's what it doesn't liberate you from: the liquor cabinet, the hospital, and an early grave. Incredibly, women go along with the healthy at any size movement despite seeing its proponents drop dead from heart attacks or suffering all sorts of other obesity-related conditions.

The only explanation for such blindness in the face reality is that they just don't care. They're happy to embrace their inner Orca. And the saddest part is that they're perfectly willing to encourage their "sisters" toward wanton self-destruction too, so long as they can keep shoveling food down their own gullets without a hint of restraint. It's like a mutually assured destruction society, with extra gravy.

Maybe feminists endorse keeping women fat to make them less interested in athletics. Even the fittest young women can't compete with the trannies taking over women's track and field, wrestling, weight lifting and almost every other women's sport. The destruction of women's athletics is being accomplished with the full approval of feminism by the way. I know—what a shock!

Feminism and its allies in the L.G.B.T. empire (too numerous to list) have attacked feminine virtues almost to the extent they've attacked masculine virtues. A young woman not interested in S.T.E.M. is seen as somehow less of a woman—submissive and weak— unless of course she is a gender studies major. Not choosing the right major is bad enough, but imagine the pressure put on young women who aren't interested in college, nor in working 40 hours a week in an office until they've wasted their most fertile, most productive years.

If you're a young woman reading this, you don't need to imagine the pressure, it has to be so overwhelming I don't know how you poor dears cope. Sadly, tragically, too many cope by indulging in comfort eating, or in meaningless, licentious sex, neither of which offer even short term relief, nor do anything to fill the long-term void which will inevitably be left by your lack of children and a deeply meaningful committed relationship.

While that is happening, Hollywood is churning out entertainment that either portrays women as stand-ins for crass teenage jerks or boosts up female characters in such a ham-fisted and unlikeable manner that even young girls don't identify with the characters.

Here's a red pill for the ladies—those movies and shows are written by male feminists who think you'll fuck them for writing a "powerful" woman, or at least get you in a position where they can rape you. Your support of films and TV shows featuring women's "empowerment" is like chum in the water. Quit inviting the sharks in closer, for fuck's sake.

The modern unlikeable women characters are known as a "Mary Sue," in short, an invincible woman with no weaknesses. Think about some broad piloting the Millennium Falcon better than Han Solo, or a superheroine more powerful than all the Avengers put together. This isn't empowering to women, it's ruinous to good story telling. Go back to my amazing *Ghostbusters* review for a primer on an excellent female character. The horrific monstrosities in *Ghostbusters* were the two-dimensional characters and their one-dimensional dialogue, so I explained what a real heroine looks like:

> *Compare the female* Ghostbusters *with my favorite female character of all time,* Buffy the Vampire Slayer. *Buffy's feminine qualities are part of her strength. She saves the world using her female vulnerability, not in spite of it. In fact, her femininity is the only thing that makes her capable of heroic feats.*[7]

What can you learn from *Buffy the Vampire Slayer*? Feminine virtues are a strength! Pop culture and globalists may want you to be an office drone sliding into alcoholism as you binge Netflix in your husbandless, childless apartment, but you don't have to accept this fate!

Once you make the determination not to try to mimic male-to-female trannies, a whole new set of options opens itself to you. You're already completely screwed with the supposed sisterhood of feminism, why don't you try taking up the activities they consider "beneath" modern women? Skills like sewing, cooking, keeping a clean house, caretaking, and of course mothering. All these things disgust feminists but attract masculine men who desire fem-

---

[7] https://www.breitbart.com/tech/2016/07/18/milo-reviews-ghostbusters/

inine qualities as much as you desire masculine qualities in them.

In short, if you play the feminist game, don't be shocked if a soy boy has you pinned down after spiking your drink. It's likely the only way he's getting a leg over, after all. And masculine men would rather go without than have sex with a feminist, so that's the best you'll get. If you embrace feminine virtue, the male feminist will not only despise you, they'll fear you like the pussies they are.

This may be a lonely road at first. Many of your friends will reject you for not buying into feminism's nightmare vision of your future. Guess what, those bitches were never your friends. This is much harder for women than men—but over time, some of your female friends will come to the same conclusion you have. They'll burn their pussy hats and magically remember your phone number. It's up to you if you let them back in your life—you'll be busy with new friends and most likely the man of your dreams and a passel of lovely children.

You might be tempted to show off the goods as you get in shape with revealing tops and the ubiquitous yoga pants that every woman seems to wear, especially if they don't have the body to pull them off. (Spandex is a privilege, Ladies. Not a right.) I'd counsel you to exercise restraint and decorum. Modesty is a feminine virtue, and I don't think that expecting a virtuous woman to wear clothing in public rather than lingerie is akin to putting them in a burka.

On a personal level, I'm tired of throwing up in my mouth every time I'm walking behind a chubby girl wearing pants so tight, she could get a gynecological exam without undressing.

In everything you do, remember that feminine virtue isn't what's being sold to you by Netflix, or feminists on campus, or anyone else who is— mysteriously—still single, childless, miserable, and who's most successful relationship happens to be with her cat. Don't let these people sell you on their version of what it means to be a woman like them. Fat, unattractive, angry, bitter… and alone.

Feminine virtue is timeless and must be protected. Like it or not, you live in an age in which you need to first sort yourself out, and then prove to the men who have sorted themselves out that you aren't one of the witches out to destroy them. I have a lot more advice for my female readers, but I'm cutting it off here, at roughly 80 per cent the length of the men's chapter. The gender wage gap may be a hoax, but the gender Milo gap is real. Sorry ladies. Bros before hoes.

HOW TO TALK TO EACH OTHER

Once you've made the decision to reclaim your gender—one of the two that exist—you can move on to tackling the next major problem in life, talking to the opposite sex. I don't plan to solve the communication issue in a single chapter here... think of all the relationship therapists, authors, and experts I'd put out of work! But I do have a lot of insight and tips for straight people to bridge the daunting, and ever-growing, chasm between men and women. Anything less wouldn't be MILO.

Communication and relationships between the sexes are so complicated, they are the one thing that used to make me thankful to be gay. Talking with other gay guys is simple. It usually boils down to putting down every woman and other homo in the room, including each other, then discussing where to score drugs and where to fuck. Post-coital pillow talk is simple and refreshingly uncomplicated: just "Don't hit me again," or "Please just take my wallet and don't hurt me."

Being gay gives me a unique perspective on communication between the sexes. I can talk to men either as potential sexual partners, in a sense playing the role of a woman, or as platonic friends, the role of a man. I can speak to women as friends—women love gay guys because we aren't thinking about having sex with them every three seconds, so we're the "safe" men to be around. Gays and women often have their own intrasexual competition dynamic as they compete for beefcake, but I've rarely experienced that. Sorry darlings, I love you, but you're not in my league.

If you can find a bookstore that is still open for business, you'll find a gigantic section devoted to communication with the opposite sex. A lot of these books are traps. They are designed to sell copies, not solve problems, so they tend to introduce a significant confirmation bias into the equation. Women buy relationship books, so in what shouldn't be a shocker, relationship books say women are great and it's all the man's fault.

If I asked you to name a relationship book off the top of your head, the title that would probably come to mind is John Gray's classic, *Men are from Mars, Women are from Venus*. I haven't read the book. I'm a faggot, but not a total queer. There is a literal truth in the title however: when women speak to men, they feel starved for life-giving attention and chilled by the lack of emotion, as if they were wandering around in Mars' paper-thin atmosphere. On the other hand, when men speak to women, they feel like they are burning in hell for all eternity, as if they were experiencing Venus's 872-degree surface temperature.

What *Men are from Mars* does get right is that there exists a fundamental divide in communication between men and women. This difference isn't insurmountable, but most people seem unaware of it, and go through life wondering why they can't communicate with the opposite sex. The difference can be summarized as what we say, and what we mean.

Men typically say what they mean, while women often expect others to use context clues and emotional intelligence to figure out their meaning. This can be summarized in the stereotypical situation where the wife asks the husband "Do these pants make my ass look fat?" and he knows he's fucked before he opens his mouth. (Incidentally, if I ever ask you if my ass looks fat, the correct answer is "Yes.")

In my extremely short summary of the problem, you should already see multiple red flags. Men say what they think, even if that is hurtful. Women expect men to use emotion to understand them, when most men hardly understand the emotion they experience directly. This fundamental difference spirals out of control as it begins to apply to the different aspects of a relationship.

For example, men and women argue and wage war differently. Men wage war with weapons, a physical affair. Women wage war with words. When it comes to words, the masculine is not to take it personally, while women take everything to heart. Look, I'm with you sisters, for me words cut deeper than any knife, but I'm gay, and straight men should not act like gay guys.

One of the reasons our world has spiraled out of control and begun turning into shit is the feminization of culture on this subject. Young people are being indoctrinated at college that words are violence, that free speech is assault. They believe they are completely justified in physically attacking speakers, because in their minds, they are meeting violence with violence.

It isn't only at college, of course: This narrative has seen a massive push on the Internet. In the minds of the progressive pussies at Twitter, a radical feminist adopting the Milo message of "There are two genders," is equivalent to sticking a knife in the heart of a tranny.

The feminization of the Internet and the campus came with a host of new sins that straight people commit. One of my favorites is the "microaggression," because remember, the most innocuous thing you say to another person can be the equivalent of a punch to the face. I highlighted the future of communication the Left dreams of in a *Dangerous Faggot Tour* speech at the University of Washington January 2017. The title of that lecture was "Cyberbullying Isn't Real."

Consider the microaggression. It is a relatively recent creation on campus, one that essentially takes a magnifying glass to the most minor of annoyances in order to make it seem colossal. Isn't that the same thing as taking unkind words on the Internet and making a crying response video? Somehow, we transformed our culture from being based on free speech, to one full of thin-skinned babies whose feelings must be protected both on campus and online. Just think. When George Bush, Sr. ran for President, they called him a wimp! George H.W. Bush was a fighter pilot and head of the C.I.A.!

What will happen when we have the first presidential campaign featuring a genderqueer furry who has videos of himself crying on YouTube because someone insulted his My Little Pony drawings? If this keeps up, your future Commander in Chief may have a history of sexually abusing xirself *to gay* Harry Potter *fanfiction.*[8]

So, the first thing straight people can do is reject the feminization of, well... *everything.* Men, if the ugly women and limp-wristed future rapists are calling you "toxic," you're on the right track. Women: Resist the urge to join the feminization of America. Understand communication that celebrates both masculinity and femininity is the only way to go.

---

[8] https://www.breitbart.com/social-justice/2017/01/20/milowhycyberbullyingisntreal/

HOW TO BE STRAIGHT

I can hear some of you whining—which really isn't a straight thing to do by the way—that I'm addressing the subject in broad strokes instead of giving you specifics. I'd love to give you all personal counselling on communication with the opposite sex, but I doubt you can afford me. What I will do, because I love all of you, is point out some of the common mistakes men and women make about the opposite gender.

✳

And now for some tips on avoiding unnecessary warfare. Pay attention to a few simple rules and you could spare yourself 99% of tiresome domestic flare-ups—or your money back![9]

WHAT MEN ALWAYS GET WRONG ABOUT WOMEN

Women want to be treated as equals: They don't lads, they just think they do after a lifetime of feminist conditioning. Women want to be cared for and protected.

The little things don't matter: It's true, things like "anniversaries" were created by women to force men to remember things, but that doesn't make them any

---

[9] Absolutely no refunds.

less important. A good woman is worth the effort to hit the little things.

Appearance doesn't matter: When you see a hot babe with a slob, you know he's loaded or has a 12-inch dick. If he's white, you can assume it's the wallet. If you're the provider but a big slob, don't be shocked when she's checking out the pool boy.

Women don't want to "take care" of a man: Again, it's feminist agitprop. Women are nurturers and thwarting the motherly instinct even with a grown man will leave her frustrated. Just set limits, she shouldn't be changing your diapers unless that's your kink.

Women want an equal say in everything: When there is a leadership role to be taken, a man should take the responsibility. As much as women believe they want an equal partnership in everything, deep down they don't want to take certain responsibilities, that's why they have a man—so be a man!

WHAT WOMEN ALWAYS GET WRONG ABOUT MEN

Men want to know our emotions: Women really believe men want to know every nuance of their emotional state in extreme detail. Meanwhile men are chewing their leg off like a trapped animal. I'm a faggot and I'm doing the same thing!

Men should know when women are in the mood for sex: Men don't have the concept of being in the mood. We're in the mood unless we've ejaculated in the last five minutes, and even then, sometimes it doesn't matter. Straight men are in the mood regardless of if you are sweaty, if you haven't shaved your legs or pubic hair, or any other excuse you can think of. If you'll excuse me, I think I'm going to be sick.

Men are always insulting women: Women have their guard up, as they've been trained to, and perceive everything men do as an insult. Trust me, more than half the time your man not only didn't mean to insult you, he doesn't even perceive that you are insulted. Whatever it was, it wasn't personal, honey, so let's not make it World War III okay? At least until I leave the restaurant.

Women should make men choose them over other activities: Women should never make men choose spending time with them over other things they want to do. Girls, even if you "win," you end up losing because he will resent it and hold a grudge.

Obviously, this suggestion doesn't apply to making him choose you over other women, that's reasonable.

HOW TO TALK TO EACH OTHER

Let it be known far and wide, Milo has admitted
women are capable of being reasonable.

*

Some readers may have expected me to take a
purely pro-male position in this chapter, that it is
entirely women who must change their communication style to suit men. But relationships involve two
people, and both people must work together to find
common ground.

Although both sexes must work on communication and learn about how the other sex speaks, the
feminization of Western civilization is certainly one
of the major problems inhibiting that communication.

It's not that feminine communication is purely
evil—although loads of red-pilled women will tell
you that it actually is—it's that young men are forced
to adopt a feminine style of communication, which
goes against every iota of their D.N.A., hormones,
and racial memory if you're a believer in Jung's work.

HOW TO FIND LOVE

Let me tell you right from the top that this chapter will not quote from my past work, there are no Milo gems footnoted. As I worked on this book, I've put more thought into penis-in-vagina sex, and the straight relationships than surround that (gross) act, than I have during the rest of my life put together. I hope you all appreciate my sacrifices on your behalf!

The subject of straight people finding love, having sex, and building relationships is tough for me. If men are from Mars and women are from Venus, gays are from Pluto. I bet you thought I'd say Uranus, but I'm a bottom, darlings. Besides, when I have experimented with straight sex, I haven't had to work at it at all—women throw themselves at me! I'm their ideal man, which should tell you that women are not particularly logical creatures. Now, I'm not going to solve all the world's relationship problems in a few humble pages, but I'm Milo, so I'll damn well try.

The first mistake straight men make when they think about who they want to be in a relationship with is that they consult their penis instead of their head or, more importantly, their heart. I'm sure the ladies consider this a predictable problem. Straight guys when asked about their dream girl will talk about her hair color, her breast size, perhaps her sexual proclivities.

There are more important things to a relationship lads—I'm not discounting sex, but once you're in a monogamous relationship with a woman for five years, you will value other aspects of your significant other as much if not more than her cleavage, or the disgusting foldy bits of her vagina. Sorry, I sort of tuned out the whole female anatomy section of sex ed.

As an aside, this concept is uncharted waters for most gays. A typical San Francisco homo can't imagine fucking the same guy twice in a five-year period, let alone being in a monogamous relationship that long.

In their most pathetic form, straight men are so sex-starved that their only requirement is a woman that will have sex with them and keep doing so—leading to these poor souls taking all manner of abuse and accepting their woman wearing the pants in the family, a miserable fate.

Women, you don't get off scot free in the "having bad priorities" area either. Did you *honestly* think Milo would allow women go unscathed in this analysis? Bitch please. Women typically look at a guy and find basic flaws at the core of their being but believe, most likely out of hubris, that they are the ones that will "fix" this man.

They set out to fundamentally alter the man's character, habits, and life and remold them into the woman's vision of perfection. Then they are shocked when it doesn't work. Ladies—you aren't the host of a house fixer-upper show, and relationships are not the Home & Garden Network.

Both men and women must look within themselves before looking at potential partners and figure out what really matters to them. You really should complete a personal inventory—get yourself down on paper. And don't lie, you're not going to show this to anybody but yourself. If you want to lie to yourself, then not only should you drop this book right now and join the L.G.B.T.Q.+ spectrum, you probably should avoid listening to another word I ever say—your mind is better off without hearing what I have to say.

Determine for yourself what is most important in your life, and those are the items you cannot compromise on with a potential mate. For example, you are likely a very political person. You will not be happy in a relationship with a person holding the opposite convictions. We've witnessed this unfolding broadly in America and the rest of Western civilization, a schism between Left and Right—so why you'd want to bring that into your own home is beyond my ken.

You can certainly match up well with someone that is apolitical, but I believe the high-profile relationships between people bitterly divided on politics are largely a sham. I'm talking about relationships here—men, if you want to have some great sex hatefucking a radical feminist for a while, go for it! Just make sure it's videotaped for when you get the inevitable rape charge. Just understand you're risking such charges, an S.T.D., and that these flings burn out quickly and typically leave scorch marks. Don't say you weren't warned.

Other things may be more important than politics to you. Some people feel this way about religion. You may want to stay within your denomination or even within your own church. I think that is too restrictive personally, I'm happy to have a mutual faith in our Lord Jesus Christ with my husband. Never mind Catholic versus Evangelical.

I am also not opposed to mixing faiths, although there are faiths that lend themselves to each other more readily than others. In my family tree, Catholics were mounting Jews, so I can't exactly knock it, can I?

Obviously, if you are a Christian and think you'll have a happy relationship with a Muslim, you're past the point of saving. No need to mention atheists here, they make themselves unfuckable without any help from me.

A large portion of relationship fights stem from money. There are two divides on money—the first is if you grew up rich, middle class, or poor, and the second is how you spend money today. For more on money, read my book *How To Be Poor.* For our purposes here, I will say I don't believe money should be a major divide.

My husband grew up dirt poor and I certainly did not... but we are happy together regardless of my rising and falling (and rising) fortunes. After you figure out what really matters to you and what is negotiable, you can get down to work finding a good woman or man.

But where to look? This is a question for the ages. I bet the second conversation ever hard in coherent spoken language between cave men was two men saying, "I can't find a good woman, every cave is just the same thing." The first conversation, of course, started "look at the ass on Ogg's sister."

If you're a conservative and a follower of Christ, the first place to look should be a no-brainer. Find someone at church! I'm not talking about hitting on people during the sermon, churches are full of volunteer opportunities and social events designed to help you meet someone that is likely to share your worldview and hold the same things important as you. I know that as young people we always feel we have better ways of doing things, but the church has brought people together in strong relationships for a few thousand years now... it might be worth consideration.

HOW TO BE STRAIGHT

There are plenty of other places to meet a suitable person, it can happen practically anywhere. But make sure the place you are looking for love is a place where the type of person you are compatible with is likely to be found. For example, if you're going to a bar, understand who is going to be looking for a date in a bar. It's not the same person attending a church social gathering.

Above all else, making sure you're looking for a compatible person in a place where they are doing the same thing. If you want to date a dancer, don't show up at her ballet class. Look, that may seem self-explanatory, but straight men are the special needs children of the relationship world, so I've really got to spell it out clearly here.

You can also turn to online dating. Meeting someone online has some real positives. There is a chance you can get to know the other person and develop a level of friendship before you skip right to the penis-in-vagina part I was complaining about at the top of this chapter. You can certainly learn more about them than running into them in the club. The major problem with online relationships is that young people use them as a crutch to avoid relationships in real life.

Not too long ago, guys would make up a fake girlfriend that lives in another town. Now they just have an online girlfriend instead. This trap is far too easy to fall into for both men and women and must be avoided at all costs.

HOW TO FIND LOVE

Finding someone is only the beginning. There are many more variables to finding love and making it last in a stable relationship. For one thing, both men and women must reject the culture of frantic casual sex sweeping the West. The Left is using sites like Tinder to take straight sex, which is deep and sacred, and turn it into gay sex, a throwaway experience.

The criticism of elements of the far-Right, that young women sleep around and then settle on a good man once they are used up, is frequently accurate. At the same time, men are engaging in the same behavior, so they can't blame women too much for following the culture.

Casual sex won't make you happy. Gay men typically have a higher body count than the Iraq war, and I'm talking about the millions of dead Iraqis, not the thousands of American casualties. For all that sex, you'll never find a more miserable group of bitches outside of a campus feminist meeting. Men and women need to develop the discipline to keep it in their pants for a while to produce sex that's better and more fulfilling. Look, I'm doing the same thing with my husband. You won't even find me on my knees in an airport bathroom any more. Well, unless we're traveling together.

Even if you aren't jumping each other's bones, the element of attraction must still be there. That's part of the reason I've urged both men and women to get in shape. Attraction goes far beyond physical appearance of course, so learn a bit of psychology and what makes the opposite sex tick. Women like a little whiff of danger in their man.

This doesn't mean that every guy should fake being a badass, but you can figure out how to be a bit dangerous, perhaps by reading my *New York Times* bestseller, *Dangerous*. Don't come off as too dangerous, or you'll only attract the gays. I once knew a gay guy who couldn't get off unless there was a knife at his neck. No, it wasn't me, smartass.[10]

Men prefer some mystery in their women. Some gals are lucky enough to have a bit of the exotic to them thanks to ethnic heritage, but there is an easy way for any woman to be a bit mysterious—wear modest clothing. Trust me, I'm not going full Muslim on you here, and I will not be selling Milo hijabs anytime soon, but there is something to be said for covering up. You don't need to have your tits hanging out all over social media and your ass in skintight yoga pants.

Make the guys use their imagination about your curves, it will drive them wild. Ultimately, your goal is a happy, successful, and stable relationship. The way to achieve those goals, no matter what the media, Internet, and college tells you—despite even what you've perhaps witnessed in your own parents'

---

[10] It was totally me.

relationship—is to get married and have children. Preferably Christian babies in large number.

As a huge and ever-growing body of evidence shows us, pursuing a hedonistic life filled with wine and travel will include some happiness, but not the sort of long-term happiness and satisfaction that a family brings. Everyone on the Left lies about this, and most people don't learn how wrong it is until it's too late and they are bitter old hags.

This is truly revolutionary stuff for a gay guy to be telling you, but I didn't earn my title of Dangerous Faggot by telling you what the Left wants you to hear.

RAISING CHILDREN

So, let me get this straight, pun intended: you thought I had the balls to lecture straights on both communication between the sexes and finding love, but not the chutzpah to instruct you on the finer points of raising children? Oh honey, I thought you knew me better than that! There are many facets to having a successful life as a straight person but having children and properly raising them must be near the top in terms of importance.

Out of all the advantages to the straight life I've considered over the years, siring my offspring has always been the most important thing to me. And please, don't say a word about wanking off in some clinic so that a lesbian can squirt my Milo essence into herself with a turkey baster. It's not going to happen.

This isn't a new position for me. During a speech at the University of Texas, I was asked by a young gay fan if I was setting a bad example for gay Americans by saying I'd be straight if I could. In retrospect, I had nothing to worry about. I've received over the years hundreds of private communications from young gay people who told me I have either outright saved them from suicide or have given me the courage to confront the demons in their lives. Here is how I answered the student questioning my yearning for a straight pill:

> Well if I were to take a straight pill my career would be over, but I think I probably would, and I'll tell you why. And I've never really heard this from other gay people, but it always seemed perfectly obvious to me. It's not about bigotry or homophobia, because we could live in a perfect society, and in many ways we pretty much do, where people are not discriminated against on the basis of their sexuality, but for me and it might be [too much information] for some of you, but for me not being able to create a child with the person you love, you know, while you're loving them, that gets you. You notice that.[11]

I won't say having kids is the only thing that matters in life, but it is one of the most important things. Something I won't experience, at least as directly as you can as a straight person. Based on this fact, I can say with authority that you shouldn't squander your

[11] https://www.breitbart.com/social-justice/2016/09/20/milo-i-would-take-a-straight-pill/

chance to do it right. Don't miss your window to have children, as many women are when they wake up one day in their sterile office cubicles forty years old and childless.

I will not spend a lot of time in this chapter examining the major cultural push from Leftists for white Americans to not have children. Whether they say it is for the environment or any other reason, they transparently want the white people of the West to stop breeding. Perhaps I will write about this in *How To Be White* if all of you keep supporting these books.

The art of parenting is under just as intense an assault by the Left. Look, they are very happy for you to not parent your children, so they can be properly molded by schools, universities, and feminism to hate America, hate men, and hate whoever else the Left chooses to target. Some of you in the back of the class are likely asking why parenting is so important that it deserves its own chapter.

Go ahead and re-read chapter one. The rest of the class will wait. Your parents fucked you up, leaving you with a choice. Do you want to fuck up the next generation? This is what the Left wants and what human behavior dictates—a vicious cycle of bad parenting, like when abuse victims go on to abuse others themselves.

The Left tries to convince you that the unbroken vicious cycle is the only path—but life is full of options. You can choose to be a good parent, taking the best aspects of what your parents did for you, and replacing all the rot. Not only will you produce great children, but you'll piss off the Left just by existing! Every Twitter blue checkmark will tweet "We need to talk about how the nuclear family is an expression of white supremacy" while serving you in the coffee shop they work at after getting laid off from their blogging gig.

There's one key part of that mock tweet I want you to pay attention to—the nuclear family. Proper parenting requires the influence of both a father and mother, each playing a unique role, emphasizing different traits and offering complementary strengths to their children depending on their gender. The Left loves parents of single-parent households because they fail to gain an education in the virtues of both genders.

Consider the situation of black Americans, where the nuclear family was destroyed by the Left. About 70 per cent of black children are born out of wedlock according to the C.D.C. How is that working out for black America?[12]

Boys learn a great deal from their mothers, especially about emotion. But boys desperately need a father to learn masculinity. Other male role models can contribute to this, but no man can truly replace a

---

[12] https://www.cdc.gov/nchs/data/nvsr/nvsr67/nvsr67_08-508.pdf

boy's father. Mentorship is a masculine male virtue—teaching a younger man the ways of the world and setting them on the right path.

Fatherhood is the ultimate form of mentorship. When boys are raised by a single mom, or the Left's wet dream household of two lesbians, they grow up with a twisted sense of masculinity, often surrounded by manhaters. It's practically a foregone conclusion that if these boys don't turn into school shooters, they will at least mix with the wrong crowd, be it gangs or cliques of gay alt-righters.

What boys lose when their dads aren't in the picture, or ignore them, is an education in the positive aspects of masculinity. These boys have the aggression, competition, and indeed violence of masculinity, but lack their positive counterparts. Patience, discipline, sacrifice, and forbearance are learned from the father, or not until later in life. Consider basic training, where the drill instructor becomes a surrogate father for many fatherless young men.

Fathers should also play an important role in raising their daughters. Men can teach their daughters what a good man looks like, and what their expectations as women should be. Even in the strongest nuclear families, many fathers have checked out of this role almost completely—a grave mistake made by men who have bought into society's push for "fierce independent girls." Girls need to learn what a good man is, not their mother's definition of a good man, which is twisted, like most of women's perception of masculinity. Sorry ladies, no offense, but it's true.

As I said earlier, the pressure from society is on being a bad parent. Concentrating on your own desires, your own pleasures, and leaving it up to the state to raise your kids. Who has time to deal with brats after both parents spent a full day in the office, ate a junk food dinner, and just want to chill out? Plop them in front of the T.V. (or their tablet) and just get through another day until you're ready to drop them off at daycare the next morning.

Being a good parent is not as hard as you think. And don't worry, I'm not operating flying blind here—I've known and worked with some good parents who have demonstrated how to raise kids, and I've become one of the world's leading experts on bad parenting by talking to many thousands of fans now busy fixing their parent's mistakes. The most important trick to becoming a good parent is balancing your level of involvement. This should be a constantly sliding scale by the way—you need to be more involved when children are small and give them breathing room as they get bigger.

One of the most common mistakes parents make with small children is giving them too much time with electronic devices. Compared to the days of V.H.S. tapes and D.V.D.s, you have very little control over what the tykes are spending hours watching. If they're on the YouTube Kids app, they are likely see-

70

ing bizarre fetish cartoons of their favorite characters being killed or "inflated."[13]

Why not skip the messy psychological indoctrination and buy them baby's first fursuit before they can even talk? That way you'll at least have a say in their fursona. (If you don't know what those words mean, keep it that way.)

Likewise, control your own screen time! You don't want your child's memories of big events being that they sang the song or hit a homer only to look up to see daddy hunched over his phone like always. Every scintilla of attention you pay to a small boy or girl is worth its weight in gold as you both age.

Don't be afraid to speak straight with your children, they are subjected to Leftist indoctrination from an early age, so they need your viewpoint too. Teach them when they should speak up and when they shouldn't, what in their education is purely bullshit, and how to tell real news from fake news. In short, if you purchased this book, you likely developed survival skills for living in a Leftist world— don't leave your kids to figure it out all by themselves as you did. Save them a decade of pain by helping them to develop their survival skills yourself.

Finally, and perhaps most crucially, always fight the instinct to be a helicopter parent. Yes, the ed-

---

[13] https://www.engadget.com/2018/03/23/youtube-still-plagued-disturbing-kids-videos/

ucational establishment, the political establishment, and practically every facet of entertainment and the Internet wants to break your kids down into liberal zombies, but they need a bit of freedom to learn their own path as well. After all, children of over-protective parents are often soft and afraid of their own shadow, does that sound like your end goal?

Both boys and girls need some freedom to explore their world and should be fully expected to pick up some bumps and bruises along the way. They need your guidance and advice, but not your surveillance. Just because Big Tech is constantly infringing on your privacy doesn't mean you need to do the same thing to your kids, unless they give you good reason of course.

I'm not advocating against rules. Strong rules against drugs and other behavior that can destroy (or end) your child's life are simple common sense. I'm advocating against a list of rules to rival the I.R.S. tax code and removing every shred of their privacy in the process.

If you take this advice to heart and take the time to review what your parents did both well and poorly in your childhood, you are in a good position to raise the next generation. You'll notice I didn't mention putting your children on a steady diet of Milo talks as they become teens, but again, that's just common sense.

A GOOD LIFE

Let me share with you a little secret about most gay people. They have absolutely no idea how straight people spend their time. I firmly believe that is why so many gays and lesbians are convinced that straight men are always no more than thirty seconds away from beating the shit out of them.

They think you're bored to tears! Yes, the fact that some of them fantasize about getting the snot beat out of them contributes, but mostly they can't imagine life without the insanity of typical L.G.B.T. lifestyles.

No faking hate crimes at 3:00 a.m.? No sleeping for 48 hours straight after staying up 72 hours on a crystal meth binge? No Sunday mornings spent trying to remember your own name so you can find your way home? What do you all do while waiting to find a homo to beat up... collect stamps?!?

Of course, I have a completely different attitude about straights. Even before I met the man of my dreams and settled down, I recognized what makes straights great. Children are an important part of being straight, but far from the only piece of the puzzle. You can build a good life, a life that gays are simultaneously very jealous of and despise. Like having children, building a good life both foils the Left's plans and drives them fucking nuts so really, what more motivation do you need darlings?

Building a good life is about moving forward in multiple areas of your life over time. The emphasis here is placed on building—some people think of the good life as winning the lotto and having no concerns, but lotto winners usually go broke again. By building first a strong foundation and then a sturdy structure over a period of years, you'll develop a truly good life.

The alternative is what the Left desires for you—floating by in life from diversion to diversion, earning just enough to eat unhealthy foods every day and afford a data plan to watch anime. I'm talking about living with a purpose instead of just surviving day to day. I'm not knocking survival—I've had periods in my own life where that was questionable—but as I discuss in *How To Be Poor*, that survival mode should be a short-term situation, not a multi-decade lifestyle.

This, too, is impossible for the typical gay to understand. They can't imagine living to 30, let alone building a life over decades. I didn't think I'd reach that age myself, but once I did, I knew it was time to get my beautiful ass in gear. A good life is much easier to achieve if you are on good financial footing. While *How To Be Poor* is loaded with information on this topic, I'll share some suggestions here.

Firstly, find a career that is fulfilling and pays well. If you are pursuing higher education, there are several careers I find acceptable based on your sex. Men should be engineers, doctors, lawyers, or journalists. I don't mean soy boy bloggers of course; I mean real journalists. Women should be teachers, librarians, run the Parent-Teacher Association, and of course be mothers.

That is not to say that higher education is necessary. Many of the kindest people, the most grounded people really, are those that have built careers for themselves in the trades, in factories, or even driving a truck. These people are feared and despised by the globalists, who tried to destroy them through the stealing of American jobs and the proliferation of opioids.

My point is if you are in college and you don't have one of those careers in mind, are you truly setting yourself up for a good life? I think it's an uphill battle, but I'm sure your professors and the administrators counting your tuition payments would disagree!

Possessions are a big part of life. Anyone who scoffs at that and calls you a materialist is a liar trying to virtue signal. Part of living a good life is building up the right kind of possessions, like a nice car or two, appropriate furnishings, and a wardrobe. One of the keys to living the good life is not buying things you can't afford.

That Rolex watch may impress people at first glance, but as soon as they know you put every penny you have into it, it suddenly becomes less a status symbol and more a symbol of you trying too hard to impress. Americans fall into this trap with cars because of the country's fetishization of the automobile. Wonderful, get your expensive car, but if you're eating ramen noodles every night to make the car payment, are you really getting ahead?

A note on wardrobe. This is a critically important component of your possessions that straight men are increasingly ignoring. Perhaps due to gay men's obsession with couture and stylish clothing, straight men have become repelled by the concept of having a good wardrobe of nice stylish clothing.

Apparently, having more than three pairs of shoes is considered gay to a lot of men, who as we've previously discussed, have clung to the Homer Simpson mockery of masculinity. A straight man's wardrobe should not be jeans and cargo pants paired with tee shirts and polos. Straight men need to get back to the dapper style icons of yesteryear, like Cary Grant.

Women love a well-dressed man, and a nice wardrobe will likely inspire young women to put away the yoga pants and sports bras in favor of dress clothes as well. Quirky YouTuber TheReportOfTheWeek, better known as Reviewbrah, garners large amounts of female attention as an undersized fast food aficionado wearing suits from the thrift store. Imagine what you can do with a nice blazer?

If you need help getting started with your wardrobe, find a gay guy you trust. We gays are the only humans who innately understand how to dress men. Women will either dress you in their own personal twisted vision of how a man should look or dress you poorly in the hopes of keeping other women from sniffing around.

The ultimate purchase in your life is likely to be your home—"mortgage" means death pledge after all. When you buy a house, make sure you can handle the payment, and prepare for emergencies like a job loss. Crucially, you are likely to purchase a house with a spouse.

Don't do this lightly, because if you divorce, the house will complicate things and you may find your-self sitting in a shitty apartment contributing to the mortgage on a house loan for the place you walked in on your significant other banging your neighbor. You'll notice I wrote this neutrally, but let's be honest, in a divorce, it's almost always the man getting fucked out of the good life.

Working and buying things are only two parts of life. To globalists and gays, they are the most important things in the world, because both enrich them. Gays are, after all, the world's perfect consumers. High disposable incomes and no one important to spend their dosh on—corporate America's wet dream customer.

What about how you spend your downtime? We already know you're exercising and watching movies and T.V. shows that don't constantly vilify straight people. If you're a young person, you're probably playing video games. I will never tell you not to play video games, but my advice is to moderate the amount you play.

Games tend to suck you in to long play sessions that eat up all your free time. That isn't a problem in bursts but can be in the long term. How long before you skip the gym for another round of Fortnite or whatever the game of the month is?

You need to develop some hobbies that contribute to your masculine or feminine virtue. Men, you need to get into hiking, camping, fishing, and hunting. Developing even a modicum of self-sufficiency is extremely masculine. You don't need to go full hillbilly here, but every man should have a bit of that culture built into him. Women, you should be taking up cooking and crafts. The only young women that know how to sew clothing are cosplayers making big bucks from thirsty men on Patreon. Even if you don't want to dress up like anime characters, think of the usefulness of knowing your way around a needle and thread.

The good life goes beyond yourself. Consider spending some hours weekly on a charity or church project. Help improve those around you and improve yourself at the same time. Instead of being the guy or gal at a charity to work off community service hours, be the guy or gal at a charity to help improve the lives of those around you.

Along the same lines, if you don't have kids, find a young person that you can mentor. Teach life skills to those born into less fortunate situations. In short, be a person that contributes to society instead of someone that takes from society. And don't expect to be properly thanked for your efforts, but you should never do things just for the thanks… that's queer.

Everything discussed in this chapter contributes to turning your life from a mere matter of survival and consumption to a bigger thing, a lasting contribution to the world that you are remembered for. Your time on Planet Earth doesn't have to be a slog to a job you hate just to (barely) afford eating and drinking and diversions to take your mind off work.

You can, with effort, live a much better lifestyle, but the Leftists would prefer you didn't. They want you dumb, fat, and easy to manipulate. It's up to you if you play along, but if I were you, I'd tell them to fuck off. It worked for Trump!

FEMINISM IS CANCER

If I were writing under a slave labor contract like the old days, I'd fulfill the clause of the agreement calling for a chapter on feminism by leaving it at those three words and moving on to chapter nine. It would be hilarious to the readers and a big middle finger to my paymasters.

But I work for you, and while it would be funny, it's a better use of our time to point out why feminism is so terrible. In case you're interested, my other option for a joke chapter was to just repeat "feminism is cancer" 500 times. Sort of like *The Shining*, except in this case you'd be rooting for me to chop the fat bitches into little pieces.

Most of the book up to this point is has been about improving yourself and finding the keys to building a good life as a straight person, by embracing masculine and feminine virtue as appropriate. This chapter is different—we're going to talk about the other side now... the disgusting harpies of feminism and their male feminist allies. Let's just call male feminists what they are—rapists and sex pests. As a rule of thumb, when a man declares he is a male feminist, you can start the clock on the rape charge. I might call that "Milo's First Law of Male Feminism."

This chapter will give you some brief insights into what you should most be concerned about with feminism, but it will by no means be exhaustive. Fittingly, this is the fattest chapter in this work. I'm happy to report that I have a full book coming shortly titled *Feminism is Cancer*. It will collect my many years of slaying feminism into a single handy package.

Feminism may have had noble goals when it started, but it transformed into a terrible monster, much like most labor unions. Modern feminism was conceived as a way for fat ugly women to pull as many other women as possible down to their level—obese, unhappy, miserable in their career, and riding a rollercoaster of red wine, fatty foods, and antidepressants.

For an ideology centered on dragging women down, feminism offers two primary threats to men. Firstly, some of the more ambitious fatties had the idea of attacking the concept of masculinity along with femininity, to further hasten the downfall of Western women. It's like one of those beastly math problems where two trains are speeding towards each other, instead of one standing still. An apt analogy, because if you personally know a feminist and have had to deal with their shit for any length of time, you quickly come to wish you were standing on the tracks between those two trains.

The other threat of feminism to men is all the baggage that comes along with it. Interestingly, for a bunch of miserable women living solitary lives, their ideology is almost married to another oppressive, authoritarian ideology. Feminism's most common partner is Marxism, and even if you think feminism is a joke that will never hurt you (you'd be terribly wrong, by the way) you aren't likely to feel the same way about a bunch of freshly-minted Marxists running around town. Feminism's connection to Marxism is so easy to understand that even a feminist can get it.

Proud independent women may not need a man, but they need to eat. And judging by the size of most feminists, they need to eat a lot, and frequently. But feminists have no real-world skills, they cannot grow, kill, or even cook their own food. Therefore, they require an economic system based on taking from those who produce, and giving to those that stink... erm, to those that need. Sorry, sometimes even on my best behavior, I get away from myself.

I firmly believe that we cannot convert feminists from hysterical drones of the collective sisterhood into thinking people. Like drunks, they need to find their own bottom. For some of them that will never happen, for others they will wake up one day realizing their life choices are why they are single, miserable, and angry—not the patriarchy as they've been told.

Some wags will argue a feminist can be straightened out with a program of vigorous rutting, but I'm quite skeptical. Firstly, to attempt to mount an obese feminist white maintaining an erection is more of a kamikaze mission than any Japanese pilot ever took on. And Heaven forbid the battleship roll over on you—it's *sayonara* for sure then! Secondly, gays used to try this on me, but none of them could ever fuck the conservatism out of me.

Thirdly, any feminist that is remotely attractive is already engaged in the freakiest degrading sex acts you can imagine. It's the secret fuel for their man-hating rants. For example, a certain young woman of Asian descent infamous for her anti-white tweeting—who recently picked up a cushy mainstream media gig—has never been able to keep the white boyfriend she desperately desires because she demands they dress up like soldiers and rape her at gunpoint, a scene straight out of North Korean propaganda.

I think the best course is to avoid any contact with feminists at all. It will greatly improve your life! I documented this concept in a 2015 piece titled, "Why I Will Only Sit on Straight White Male Panels from Now On."

This prohibition is especially pertinent for tech industry events, where I will now refuse to take a conference stage

*unless the panel is entirely straight, white and male.
I've had enough of diversity quotas, which only produce
idiots and a terrible experience for the audience. Look,
it's not my fault meritocracy always seems to produce
male winners.*

*You can consider my new position as a heroic stance
against the fact-free feminist loons and whinge-bag progressive diversity campaigners who say that no discussion about artificial intelligence or virtual reality can
possibly be worthwhile or interesting unless it's chaired
by a transgender Iranian Muslim with a wooden leg.*[14]

Other prominent men have come to the same conclusion. Mike Pence won't have dinner alone with
a woman besides his wife. Following the #MeToo
movement, it was widely reported that men in corporate America lost interest in mentoring young
women or even being in a room alone with them, for
fear of a sexual misconduct charge.[15]

These men have it right—dealing with feminists
involves far more risk than reward, so do whatever possible to avoid them. If you must have in-
teractions with a feminist, make sure to video the

---

[14] https://www.breitbart.com/tech/2015/10/28/why-i-will-only-
sit-on-straight-white-male-panels-from-now-on/

[15] https://www.forbes.com/sites/pragyaagarwaleurope/2019/02
/18/in-the-era-of-metoo-are-men-scared-of-mentoring-
women/#3760e2dd7d0d

encounter—even kangaroo courts on campus can't really argue against video. Of course, driving apart the sexes is one of feminism's chief goals, so the #MeToo movement can be seen as a big win for the big girls.

Men have it bad with feminism. These loathsome women and their allies in seemingly every walk of life have dedicated themselves to destroying masculinity along with femininity and reshaping to become "non-toxic" masculinity.

Their vision of how straight men should look—and act—is basically like a fat feminist but with a nine-to-five job and paycheck to hand over. They look the other way when they are joined by male feminists, because Lord knows these dumb ugly fat useless sacks of shit need all the help they can get. Beggars can't be choosers!

As I said at the outset, male feminists are typically perverts looking to get laid. If they aren't clever enough to weasel their way into vulnerable women's pants, they'll just skip straight to rape. Or they see feminism as a surface virtue to cover up their past sex crimes and degeneracy. The fat cows haven't figured this out, no matter how many of their male allies get exposed.

As bad as feminism is for men, it is much worse for women. Women lack the masculine trait of rebellion, so they are much more likely to comply with the overwhelming cultural pressure to become a feminist, or at least agree with feminist ideology—for example the gender wage gap, which is accepted as real even by many conservative women.

Young women improperly raised and left without good female and male role models are left adrift, and perfect raw materials to be chewed up and spat out by the cult of feminism. Used up women are the *only* thing ever spat out by the fat pigs of feminism. I'm talking about food of course, once they get past a certain size, they don't have to worry about a man ejaculating in their mouth.

Feminism's negative effects on women are well documented, especially in my forthcoming book *Feminism is Cancer*. But in the context of *How To Be Straight* it is vitally important to understand one of the ways that feminism destroys the lives of young women. Feminism will literally make you as ugly as the hags guiding you down their path. As every woman knows, it's all about the hormones. And feminism interferes with those hormones so severely that you will end up an ugly misshapen wreck.

It's as if the female subconscious, no doubt more rational and logical than the female conscious mind, goes on strike: "right, I'll show this daft cunt," flooding the body with testosterone and sapping it of the all-important estrogen. This sounds like something out of sci-fi, but it's unfortunately all too real. I documented some of the changes brought on by hormones in a column titled "Does Feminism Make Women Ugly?"

> *High-testosterone women are more likely to get guts be-cause it's estrogen that controls fat around the waist, hips and rear. Lena Dunham's body shape—and per-haps her behavior—would appear to be a result of very high testosterone.*
>
> *As for the other changes women go through when they discover you can make a career out of hating men, well. I can't explain why it seems as though feminist's eyes go glassy and dead the longer they are incentivized to behave like bros while sloshing about in misandry for pay. I'm sure an entertaining gallery could be assembled showing how the process takes its toll; perhaps a reader can oblige.*
>
> *But the power of hormones to radically alter physiology is well-documented. Trans patients attest to the extraor-dinary shifts in appearance and even personality that can be brought about by changes in hormone levels—as do older women on hormone replacement therapy.*[16]

No matter how hard they try, feminists cannot defeat mother nature—they still want to have sex. But feminists are ugly, and progressively get uglier

---

[16] https://www.breitbart.com/politics/2015/07/26/does-feminism-make-women-ugly/

as their hormones get further out of whack. Women and gays are already familiar with where I am going with this... ugly people have low self-esteem, and people with low self-esteem become promiscuous to compete with the beautiful people.

Promiscuous women go on birth control which... *makes them even uglier.* This is the worst vicious cycle of feminism and no one talks about it. No one, that is, except for me. I laid it all out in the tastefully titled column "Birth Control Makes Women Unattractive and Crazy." You really need to read and internalize that column, especially female readers, to understand just how terrible feminists want to make your life. Here is just a little snippet to tease you:

> *It's not just your body that will get less sexy. Your voice will lose its seductiveness too. Women sound most attractive to men when their estrogen levels are high, and their progesterone levels are low. Birth control lowers the former and raises the latter, making women sound as erotically appealing as Bruce Jenner giving a croaky acceptance speech.* [17]

Very few people (besides the Dangerous Faggot) are brave enough to take on feminism like this. That article resulted in one of my crowning achievements, when Hillary Clinton read the title as part of her

---

[17] https://www.breitbart.com/tech/2015/12/08/birth-control-makes-women-unattractive-and-crazy/

speech to demonstrate just how awful I am. It's a moment in my life I'll never forget, and I discussed it the next day at George Washington University. Here is how I described it then:

> *"She reads out with a straight face,"* continued Milo, *"with that sort of 'swallowed a lemon' kind of thing, it's just like pissing off your grandma at Thanksgiving, 'to give you a flavor of some of his work here are some of his headlines and I'm not making this up. Birth control makes women unattractive and crazy'… and her own audience burst out laughing!*

> *"Because it's so funny! Then she stumbles over the next one, 'would you rather your child had feminism or cancer!' and she's looking around the room for someone to be horrified along with her and her own audience are just like 'I gotta look this up.' "*[18]

If you take anything away from this chapter, it must be that it is not only your duty to avoid feminists whenever possible, but to reject their ideology strenuously whenever necessary. Feminists want to destroy manhood and have been successful in many cases. But that is just one step in their ultimate campaign, to destroy womanhood.

If you are a man, do you want anything to do with a woman who is part of this cult? If you are a woman,

---

[18] https://www.breitbart.com/social-justice/2016/10/21/milo-thing-hillary-likes-clamping-free-speech-scissoring/

do you want to become Hillary Clinton, or worse yet, the typical Gender Studies professor? If you don't think these options are both worse than death, I fear you might be too far gone. Try two weeks of total immersion in Milo books and videos and maybe— just maybe—you'll come to your senses.

FAGS ARE GAY

It's time for a thought experiment. I want you to imagine that you are part of a group that on average is highly intelligent, high income, good looking, and creative. In the worlds of art, entertainment, style, and nightlife, you're the cream of the crop. Now, add in the fact that you're so tremendously insecure that you're left in a puddle of emotions—literally shaking and crying—if every major brand doesn't pander to you, the crosswalks aren't rainbow colored, the police doesn't bow down to you, and you don't wield unlimited power to dictate what people and companies do and say despite their religious beliefs.

Your group believes the way to fight for your rights is to buy a Chick-fil-A meal so you can take a selfie kissing in the restaurant, and that parents must submit to having their children exposed to your drug and sex club culture. Congratulations! You've just gotten a Milo introduction to why fags are so fucking gay!

Everything I said above is true. Homosexuals are smart, typically earn big paychecks, and are the life of the party—not to mention making up the vanguard of culture. But instead of remaining a mischievous counterculture, gay culture first made the major misstep of aligning itself with the hysterical L.G.B.T. community, and then secondly decided to join in feminism's fun of dictating to straight people how to live their lives.

Maybe mainstream homos just feel the need to make their mark on culture that is beyond their talents in the arts and business. The lifestyle led by so many gays—an endless parade of strangers to fuck and drugs to snort so they can fuck again—is so unfulfilling, any person with a heart wouldn't blame me for wanting to escape it. I found my escape with my wonderful husband, but for a long time I simply hoped for a straight pill.[19]

The problem with gays is all of us—and I can't honestly exclude myself from this—are addicted to drama. When drama involves gays, women, or North Korea—what I call the Axis of Evil—it always escalates. If you give a gay eight inches, he'll take eight miles. Straights thought gays would be happy with equal rights, but instead they demanded special rights, like the right to decide where Chick-fil-A can open stores or deciding if Christian bakers have the right to not create custom wedding cakes for queers.

---

[19] https://www.breitbart.com/social-justice/2016/09/20/milo-i-would-take-a-straight-pill/

Gays have done a tremendous amount of damage to the relationship between gays and straights.

In 2015, I documented this fact in a column titled, "Dear Straight People: I'm Officially Giving You Permission to Say Gay, Faggot and Queer."

> Left-wing loons will no doubt say that I am ushering in a new era of "harassment" and "abuse." I say screw you, you ugly fat losers. Letting everyone say "queer" and "faggot" is truer to the free-thinking spirit of dissident gay culture than your odious language-policing ever has been. Let's all stick two fingers up! Up where is up to you.
>
> If there is any residual resentment directed at gays these days, it's not ordinary fags people don't like. It's the schoolmarmish bullies of G.L.A.A.D. and Stonewall and the gay establishment. Frankly, listening to their dreary pronouncements on "cis privilege" makes me want to put on a wifebeater, rent a pick-up truck and beat the living daylights out of the village twink. [20]

Until a large group of dissident gays is brave enough to come out as conservative, young gays will continue to get sucked into the left-wing L.G.B.T. combine. They think it's the only way to be gay! Corporations are happy to play along—gays are their

---

[20] https://www.breitbart.com/tech/2015/12/11/dear-straight-people-im-officially-giving-you-permission-to-say-gay-faggot-and-queer/

best customers, with high disposable incomes and no brats to divert money into college savings accounts.

They aren't worried about retirement either, no gay believes he will live past thirty. All a company must do is make a logo with a rainbow flag and tweet about loving gays throughout the month of June, and then sit back and count the profits. It's pathetic once you understand what's really going on.

I wrestled with talking about gay kids in the parenting chapter or here... I'm a faggot, you can't *really* expect me to make tough choices, can you? I finally decided on this chapter to include my most heartfelt and difficult message. Parents, you must do whatever is within your power to keep your children from going gay.

It is an unhappy existence, and as parents you should desire your offspring to have a real shot at a happy and fulfilling life. The Leftists say the exact opposite—they want every kid in the West on the L.G.B.T. spectrum and append a new letter to the acronym every day to suck another hapless child into the cult.

Gays are only part of the problem. The rest of L.G.B.T. culture is much worse. Starting with lesbians, who are largely responsible for radical feminism too. Thanks, ladies! If it's any comfort, the rug munchers who taught women to hate men are collectively miserable failures at life. Lesbians stop having sex so uniformly that there is a term for it—

lesbian bed death. It sounds a bit like crib death doesn't it?

Believe me, we'd all be better off if lesbians died as babies. Lesbians would benefit most of all—since they don't have sex, they make up for it by beating the shit out of each other. Domestic violence is off the charts in lesbian relationships, and studying it is taboo. Consider this eye-opening snippet from a tastefully titled column by a beautiful and insightful genius, "Attack of the Killer Dykes!"

> The Huffington Post *reported in 2014 that 50 per cent of lesbian women experience one of these Sapphic skirmishes at some point in their lives. Yet it wasn't until 2002 that researchers bothered to look into the scale and character of lesbian domestics and understanding of the phenomenon has not increased dramatically, even among lesbians themselves.*
>
> *Plus, the women who submit themselves to surveys like this tend to be white and middle-class. When you consider how much higher domestic abuse rates are among poorer communities with drug problems, the overall rate of lesbian violence is likely to be very much higher.*[21]

Young women are at terrible risk of being captured by the lesbian coven. Women's sexuality is far

---

[21] https://www.breitbart.com/europe/2015/05/07/attack-of-the-killer-dykes/

more malleable than men's, so they are at constant risk of flipping to the scissoring-squad as the relentless drumbeat of homosexuality is drilled into their brains. They don't know they are resigning themselves to a miserable and battered life where they will probably have to fake a hate crime just to get some attention.

Likewise, women are at risk of falling into the trap of political lesbianism. A sad attempt by women to reject the man that hurt them in favor of the sisterhood. It never works out for them though. If they remain sexually attractive, they have a chance of waking up and going straight again, but they usually have thrown away some of their best years on being angry lezzers, not to mention picking up a broken nose and truly heinous fashion sense.

Lesbians reject everything wonderful about women. They forcibly remove from their own makeup the feminine virtues I spent a whole chapter talking about. Why gays have joined forces with lesbians is simply beyond me. Lesbians are never as smart, successful, or vibrant as gays. Maybe fags like them so they can always know they are the hot one.

In L.G.B.T. culture, bisexuals are the least offensive. I used to consider bisexual men to just be confused homos. After all, if you ever lust after cock, your case for being into women is weak. Now I'm okay with my bi brethren, because they live a lifestyle much closer to how gays should be—one foot in the closet.

Bi men are much more likely than gay men to have a family, a massive loss for gays thanks to gay rights. I explained it all in "Gay Rights Have Made Us Dumber, It's Time to Get Back in the Closet." Consider my wisdom:

> But there's a problem brewing, and it has to do with evolution. In the 1950s, gay men would "live a lie," get married and have kids. They'd let off steam in dark rooms and bathhouses. That's not happening any more: the gay rights movement has liberated queens from societal expectations, so they shack up with their boyfriends and either don't have children or adopt.

> With the result that an entire generation's worth of artists, playwrights, scientists, and fashion-forward gay BFFs are being mopped up by horrified housekeepers instead of being born.[22]

So, my advice to gay men is simple: Make Gays Closeted Again. The bisexuals can do it, and they are the closest thing to a gay man there is.

Of course, no discussion of L.G.B.T. insanity can be complete without discussing the trannies. I'm going to keep it short, because I feel like this is an uplifting and positive book, and nothing could be grimmer than the transsexual movement, especially as it pertains to children.

---

[22] https://www.breitbart.com/politics/2015/06/17/gay-rights-have-made-us-dumber-its-time-to-get-back-in-the-closet/

Allow me to summarize transgender culture as it exists today. Imagine an extremely un-feminine lunatic walking around all day holding a gun to his head. As he encounters individuals and organizations, he threatens to pull the trigger and blow his brains out unless they do exactly what he wants them to do.

Despite this perpetual coercion based on a threat of suicide, no one takes steps to end the situation. No one grabs the gun or talks him into dropping it, no one takes him into custody, and no one gets him the mental health treatment he so desperately needs.

Instead, everyone bends over backwards to accommodate him—preventing his suicide for just one more day. These accommodations include allowing him to go to the bathroom with little girls, destroying women's sports by letting men win the events, and even pretending he is a woman after paying for expensive genital mutilation surgery.

Somehow, we've topped the inbred bastard Muslims cutting off girl's clits by having doctors—medical doctors for Christ's sake—that specialize in cutting off dicks and turning them into nightmare hell-spawn faux-vaginas. As if real squishy bits weren't bad enough, we're creating Frankenfannies. Abominable.

It sounds batshit crazy when I write it that way, but it is a realistic description of where we are today. Oh, there is one additional wrinkle—it's being done to children now. If a six-year-old boy—far before the age where sexuality kicks in—thinks wearing a dress is fun occasionally (and who doesn't), his mother will rush to get him started on hormones to be America's next great tranny. Ruining his entire life to gain some virtue points with the Left… it boggles the mind.

I don't consider L.G.B.T. people to be my tribe. I abandoned that ship long ago. Or more accurately, they abandoned me. The rainbow army is accepting of any variation of kink, but Heaven forbid they are forced to speak to a conservative or count us among them.

If I were part of the L.G.B.T. club, I'd strongly argue to "drop the T." I explained my reasoning in a column called "I Am So Done With The Trans Outrage Brigade: Why I'm Supporting 'Drop The T.'" I wrote this in 2015, and even though that was only a few short years ago, the trannies of yesteryear seem perfectly quaint by today's standards. Here is the crux of my argument:

And before you consider me mean or rude for trying to eject trans people from our club, note that they started it: it's trans campaigners trying to eject feminists from feminism and no-platform lesbians who don't support their every barmy pronouncement, branding them "Terfs." The trans lobby essentially wishes to shut down free speech for anyone who doesn't get on board the crazy train with a combination of social censure, lawmaking and outright vicious bullying.

Thanks to the trans lobby, we're in a world where a U.C.L.A. newspaper has to apologize for saying that women menstruate, but anyone who dares point that out is in for a nasty surprise on social media.[23]

Maybe after we drop the T, we can drop the L, and gay men can get on with the business of debauchery (while procreating as they did in the past). Until then, it is up to you, the straight people of the free world, to recognize L.G.B.T. insanity, to never bend the knee to it, and for God's sake, keep your children free of it.

Whatever you do, no matter what else you take from this chapter, never, ever allow yourself to be tempted to dabble in lesbianism. It's the most guaranteed route to misery I know.

---

[23] https://www.breitbart.com/politics/2015/11/10/i-am-so-done-with-the-trans-outrage-brigade-why-im-supporting-drop-the-t/

HOW TO DIE

My plan for this book was to be nine chapters. Look at all the ground we've covered! I've shared my thoughts on how to be a good man or woman, how to raise your children, and how to build a good life. I've also warned against feminism and its enablers in the L.G.B.T. community who want to destroy everything that makes Western civilization strong and successful.

I was ready to send this manuscript off to the publisher, when it hit me like a bolt of lightning—this Milo masterpiece is incomplete. I realized that I need to help you understand how to die.

Everyone dies. It's one of God's laws that even I can't break. We also don't get to choose how we die. You may go on the toilet like Elvis or be hit by a bus during your morning jog. This chapter isn't to instruct you on how you should kick the bucket, but instead on how to create a legacy.

Feminists live such a solitary existence, the only reason their rotting, cat-chewed corpses are even found is that they live in cheap apartments and eventually the stench of death supersedes the stench of a living cat-lady, so the neighbors notice. Gays on the other hand expect to die young and are so entrenched in the ephemeral that they don't think twice about their legacy.

To use one of the delightful American idioms I learned during my college tour, the lives of Leftists are like a fart in a windstorm. Here today, gone tomorrow. You, as a proper-thinking straight person, can build a legacy that will far outlast your time on this Earth.

The first thing to consider is that you are likely to live a long life. Without the "die young and leave a beautiful corpse" attitude of gays, or the "eat everything and leave a bloated corpse" attitude of feminism, combined with breakthroughs in medicine, you could hit 100 years old if you play your cards right.

It is up to you to act when you are young to not only keep yourself healthy, so the last ten years of your life aren't spent in a wheelchair, attached to an oxygen tank and wearing a diaper. You also need to save money for retirement, so you don't spend your twilight years working in a halal meat market in the Islamic section of Brooklyn.

Leftists want you to spend all your money today, so you have no choice but to embrace the state and suckle at the government's teat. This is a stupid plan—social security will be dead and buried long before you need it. Funding your own future is necessary before you can begin to think about building a legacy.

Philanthropy and charity are certainly one path towards a legacy. You might one day have a college building named after you. Of course, it must be one of the hard sciences or the business building. I may one day fund a public bathroom on some campus—maybe U.C. Berkeley—called the Milo Center for Gender Studies. It's the only way I can imagine making that subject even more full of shit than it already is.

When a person dies with significant assets, they pass on a very tangible form of legacy in the form of their estate, distributed as they see fit. You may give a leg up in life to your children or help someone who has dealt with bad breaks in life. You might also help fund the career of your favorite dashingly handsome Dangerous Faggot. Listen, I'm not hoping for you to die, but it wouldn't be the worst idea to tell an ailing rich relative how awesome I am, would it?

Your financial legacy is also an excellent way to give a final fuck you from beyond the grave to whichever relative treated you terribly in life. If daughter #2 turned feminist, write her out of the will! When she learns she gets nothing, she'll cry real tears, as opposed to the crocodile tears she shed at your funeral.

Of course, charity comes into play at your death as well. Unlike feminists who donate to their local cat rescue at death, you have the chance to change lives for the positive as you shuffle off this mortal coil. Choose wisely, and your dollars will save lives long past your death.

Our culture works hard to convince you that life is only about the material world. What you own, who sees you wearing expensive clothing—suffice to say that I've been there, done that. But your legacy goes far beyond material wealth and possessions.

How do you want to be remembered? You should work to be remembered as a helpful, virtuous person. Spend your life helping others, doing the right thing, and supporting God and country and you'll go down in the books as a good guy. They may not sing songs about you or write books about your life—most people don't get that treatment—but if you live on in the memory of even one person, your legacy is secured, and you've achieved something akin to immortality.

At the same time, never let false legacies foisted on us by the Left get you down. Take for example Che Guevara, whose face is on a shirt in the closet of every Leftist dipshit in America. Never mind that he was a murderous commie asshole who hated gays and blacks—he's an icon of the Left. But we know the truth about him, and we know he is burning in hell for eternity with Castro, Mao, and all their communist friends.

HOW TO DIE

I've purposefully left the Bible out of most of this book because I didn't want to overload anyone with religion on top of advice that contradicts everything our culture tells you about being a straight person. But I'd like to close with a Bible verse that instructs Christians how to live a good life and leave an honorable legacy.

I also believe it fits brilliantly with the theme of *How To Be Straight*, which is rejecting the Left's push to destroy the genders and turn straight people into drones who are capable of breeding, but who are increasingly choosing to refrain from doing so. *Romans 12:2* reads:

And be not conformed to this world; but be reformed in the newness of your mind, that you may prove what is the good, and the acceptable, and the perfect will of God.

Okay, thanks for listening, everyone. You can go back to breeding now! And: You're welcome. I love you all.

APPENDIX: MILO REPLACES
STRAIGHT PRIDE MASCOT

JUNE 7, 2019. Super Happy Fun America is proud to announce that there will be a Straight Pride Parade in Boston.

Straight Pride Boston
August 31, 2019
Time: 12 noon
Start: Copley Square
End: Boston City Hall

The event is being held to achieve inclusivity and spread awareness of issues impacting straights in Greater Boston and beyond. The positive response we have received is very encouraging and leads us to believe that one day straights will be able to express pride in themselves without fear of judgement and hate.

Due to a scheduling conflict, our former mascot [Brad Pitt] is no longer available. Not to worry:

We found someone younger, more handsome, and more in tune with the heroic masculine virtues. Milo Yiannopoulos has accepted the offer to be mascot and Grand Marshal of the parade!

Upon his appointment as Grand Marshal, Milo Yiannopoulos said: "I might technically be a sequined and perfectly coiffed friend of Dorothy's, but I've spent my entire career advocating for the rights of America's most brutally repressed identity - straight people - so I know a thing or two about discrimination.

"This parade is a gift to anyone, male or female, black or white - gay and transgender allies, too! - who will stand with us and celebrate the wonder and the majesty of God's own heterosexuality. Men: Bring your most toxic selves. Women: Prepare to burn your briefcases! Because it's great to be straight, and we're not apologizing for it anymore."

A PORTION OF THE PROCEEDS FROM
THIS BOOK HAVE BEEN DONATED TO
SUPER HAPPY FUN AMERICA

*Super Happy Fun America advocates on behalf of the
straight community, in order to foster respect and awareness
with people from all walks of life*

To learn more about Straight Pride, or to organize
an event in your city, please visit
superhappyfunamerica.com

#ItsGreatToBeStraight

ABOUT THE OKAY-FOR-A-HOMO
AUTHOR OF THIS BOOK

Milo Yiannopoulos is an award-winning journalist, a *New York Times*-bestselling author, an international political celebrity, a free speech martyr, a comedian, an accomplished entrepreneur, a hair icon, a penitent and, to the annoyance of his many enemies, an exceedingly happy person. He is the most censored, most lied-about man in the world, banned from stepping foot on entire continents for his unapologetic commitment to free expression. But he is also, somehow, one of the most sought-after speakers anywhere, invited by foreign governments, wealthy individuals and even the occasional courageous private company to share his unique blend of laughter and war. Milo lurches from improbable triumph to improbable triumph, loathed by establishment Left and Right alike. His first book, *Dangerous*, sold over 200,000 copies, despite never being reviewed in any major publication. Milo lives in New Jersey with his husband, John. He loves all straight people equally.

CPSIA information can be obtained
at www.ICGtesting.com
Printed in the USA
BVHW072044050919
557647BV00002B/64/P